DINER

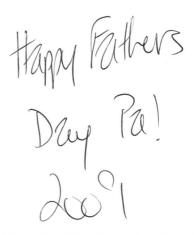

Happy Fathers
Day Pa!
2009

DINER

deliciously authentic feel-good recipes

Jennifer Joyce   photography by Martin Brigdale

RYLAND
PETERS
& SMALL

LONDON NEW YORK

First published in the
United States in 2007
by Ryland Peters & Small, Inc.
519 Broadway, 5th Floor
New York, NY 10012
www.rylandpeters.com

10 9 8 7 6 5 4 3 2 1

ISBN-10: 1 84597 381 X
ISBN-13: 978 1 84597 381 0

Senior Designer Steve Painter
Commissioning Editor
  Julia Charles
Editor Céline Hughes
Production Simon Walsh
Jacket Location Research
  Emily Westlake
Publishing Director Alison Starling

Home Economist Angela Boggiano
Prop Stylist Helen Trent
Indexer Hilary Bird

We are grateful to Starvin' Marvin's for
allowing us to photograph their diner
for our jacket, and to Lucky Seven
Diner for the inside of the book.

Starvin' Marvin's
BP Service Station
Central Parade
Western Avenue
Perivale
Greenford UB6 8TF
UK

Lucky Seven Diner
127 Westbourne Park Road
London W2 5QL
UK

Library of Congress Cataloging-in-
Publication Data

Joyce, Jennifer.
  Diner : deliciously authentic feel-good
recipes / Jennifer Joyce ;
photography by Martin Brigdale.
    p. cm.
  Includes index.
  ISBN-13: 978-1-84597-381-0
  1. Cookery, American. I. Title.
  TX715.J87 2007
  641.5'973--dc22

              2006030516

Notes
• All spoon measurements are level,
unless otherwise specified.
• Ovens should be preheated to the
specified temperature. Recipes in this
book were tested using a regular oven.
If using a convection oven, follow the
manufacturer's instructions for
adjusting temperatures.
• All eggs are medium unless
otherwise specified. Uncooked or
partly cooked eggs should not be
served to the very young, the very old,
those with compromised immune
systems, or to pregnant women.

contents

SPECIALS
Rancho Delux
Buffalo Style
Buffalo Meat Pat
Jack Chz, Onion
& BBQ Sauce
with fries £9.

introduction

Every country has restaurants that embody their culture. The British have fish and chip shops, the French bistros, and the Americans diners. American diner menus reflect the local culture and ingredients—New England has its clam chowder, Louisiana its biscuits and gravy, and Texas its chili.

Diner food is neither delicate nor fancy—it's pure comfort food. This book reflects this devil-may-care attitude but with a contemporary approach, using fresh ingredients. Although there are many recipes in this genre, I focus on the delicious classics like meatloaf, chili, and cheesecake. These are not exclusive to eating out but span generations of American home cooking.

Originally conceived as lunch wagons, diners fed hungry factory workers. Their railroad shape made them easy to tow to convenient locations until they evolved into the restaurants we have come to love. In the fifties, there were over 6,000 diners in the US. Comfy booths and long, shiny counters surrounded by chrome, spinning seats set the iconic décor. Gum-popping waitresses ("soup jockeys") poured endless refills of coffee and shouted cryptic orders using humorous and efficient diner lingo, such as "deadeye" (poached egg) and "bow-wow" (hot dog).

When I was growing up in the Midwest, eating at a diner was a big treat. I enjoyed making these recipes again, both for the irresistible food, and for the memories. I hope you enjoy them, too.

EARLY-BIRD'S BREAKFAST

The buttermilk makes these pancakes thick and fluffy. If you can't find any buttermilk, mix the same quantity of whole milk with 1 tablespoon lemon juice and let sit for 10 minutes. Be sure not to overmix the batter as the pancakes won't be as light.

blueberry pancakes

1½ cups all-purpose flour
3 tablespoons sugar
1½ teaspoons baking powder
½ teaspoon salt
3 tablespoons melted butter
1½ cups buttermilk
2 eggs, beaten
½ teaspoon pure vanilla extract
2 teaspoons vegetable oil
1 cup fresh blueberries
butter and maple syrup, to serve

serves 4

Preheat the oven to 250°F.

Put the dry ingredients in a medium bowl. Pour the wet ingredients, except the oil, into the center and mix gently. Stir until just combined.

Heat a griddle or nonstick skillet until hot. Brush the skillet with 1 teaspoon of the oil and pour about ⅓ cup of the batter into the skillet. When bubbles start appearing, sprinkle some blueberries into the pancake. Turn the pancake over and brown on the other side. Keep warm in the oven while finishing the other pancakes. Add the remaining teaspoon of oil to the pan when necessary as you make the other pancakes. Serve with butter and maple syrup.

Invest in an electric waffle iron—it's more forgiving than the stovetop equivalent. Using spray oil on the waffle iron minimizes sticking and gives the waffle a crisp edge.

buttermilk waffles with strawberries

1 cup all-purpose flour

1 tablespoon sugar

½ teaspoon salt

½ teaspoon baking powder

¼ teaspoon baking soda

1 cup buttermilk (see page 8)

1 teaspoon pure vanilla extract

⅓ cup pure vegetable oil

2 eggs, beaten

electric waffle iron or stovetop Swedish waffle iron, preheated and lightly greased

to serve

butter and maple syrup

1 cup fresh strawberries, sliced

serves 4

Preheat the oven to 250°F.

In a large bowl combine the flour, sugar, salt, baking powder, and baking soda. In a medium bowl mix the buttermilk, vanilla extract, vegetable oil, and eggs.

Pour the milk mixture into the large bowl and mix. Pour enough batter into the preheated waffle iron so that it is level at the bottom. Close the lid and cook for approximately 4 minutes, or until steam stops coming out. Don't worry if you add too much and the batter seeps out. Just wipe it clean and keep the cover closed. Keep the waffles warm in the oven while making the remainder. Serve with the butter, maple syrup, and sliced strawberries.

Ever since this egg dish began cropping up in Southwestern diners, huevos rancheros has become so mainstream it sits right next to Denver omelet on menus across the country. You can use storebought salsa for this but be sure to get the cooked variety instead of fresh.

huevos rancheros

4 corn tortillas

3 tablespoons pure vegetable oil

1 cup grated mild Cheddar cheese

4 eggs

salt and freshly ground pepper

salsa

6 plum tomatoes, halved

2 jalapeño peppers

8 garlic cloves, unpeeled

¼ cup chopped cilantro

1 teaspoon Tabasco Sauce or favorite hot sauce

1 small red onion, finely chopped, to serve

serves 4

To make the salsa, place the halved tomatoes cut side up in a shallow baking pan. Season and place on the top rack under a preheated broiler. Broil for 10 minutes, or until blackened.

Preheat the oven to 400°F.

In a dry, nonstick skillet, blacken the peppers and garlic cloves. Keep turning to color all sides. When done, peel the garlic and place in a food processor. Put the peppers in a plastic bag, tie a knot in the bag, and leave the peppers to steam for a few minutes, then peel, seed, and stem. Add the flesh to the food processor along with the tomatoes, 2 tablespoons of the cilantro and the Tabasco. Season and pulse until smooth. Pour into a saucepan and cook briefly over medium heat to warm through.

Brush the tortillas with 2 tablespoons of the vegetable oil and bake in the preheated oven for 5 minutes until golden. Divide the cheese between the tortillas and return to the oven for 5 minutes until the cheese has melted. Turn off the oven, open the door, and leave the tortillas in to keep warm. Fry the eggs in a nonstick skillet in the remaining tablespoon of oil. Place the tortillas on 4 plates and slip an egg on top of each. Spoon the warm salsa over each and sprinkle with the chopped onion and remaining cilantro.

The British invented bubble and squeak as a clever way to use leftover boiled dinner (boiled beef brisket, potato, and cabbage). Americans dropped the cabbage and renamed it corned beef hash—a savory, hearty breakfast dish.

corned beef hash

3 baking potatoes (1½ pounds), peeled and diced

3 tablespoons butter

1 medium yellow onion, diced

1 garlic clove, finely chopped

10 ounces cooked corned beef brisket, diced

½ teaspoon Tabasco Sauce

1 tablespoon pure vegetable oil

4 eggs

serves 4

Boil the potatoes in salted water for 6 minutes, drain, and put in a large bowl. Heat 1 tablespoon of the butter in a large, heavy skillet. Add the onion, garlic, and corned beef. Season and sauté for 5 minutes. Pour the mixture into the bowl with the potatoes. Add the Tabasco and mix well.

Add the remaining butter to the skillet. Pour the potato mixture into it and press everything down firmly. Cover with a heavy lid or plate that will fit just inside the skillet to weight the mixture down. Cook over medium heat for 10 minutes. Turn the mixture over in batches and cook for 10 minutes on the other side. The meat should be brown and crisp. Keep cooking and turning if it isn't. Make 4 indentations in the potatoes and crack an egg into each. Place a fitted lid over the skillet and cook until the eggs are done. Alternatively, in a separate nonstick skillet, heat 1 tablespoon vegetable oil and fry the eggs. Place one fried egg on top of each serving of corned beef hash. You can also poach the eggs instead of frying them.

SANDWICHES

The club is the ultimate sandwich; a toasted bread tower generously layered with meat, vegetables, and sometimes cheese. Mix and match with your favorite fillings.

double-decker bacon and turkey club sandwich

12 slices thick white bread

4 tablespoons mayonnaise

8 slices deli turkey

4 crisp leaves Boston or butter lettuce

1 avocado, pitted, peeled, and thinly sliced

8 paper-thin red onion slices

8 bacon slices, cooked crisp

4 beefsteak tomato slices

toothpicks

serves 4

Toast the bread, then spread one side of each piece of toast with the mayonnaise. Stack the turkey, lettuce, and avocado on 4 of these and top with another piece of toast. Stack the red onion, bacon, and tomato over and top with the remaining toast. Cut the sandwich in half diagonally and then again diagonally in the opposite direction. Secure all 4 pieces with a toothpick. Repeat with the other 3 sandwiches. Serve with Potato Salad (page 51).

My family always used to make these sandwiches with Velveeta. It melted like a dream but this grown-up version made with real cheese is even better.

best darn grilled ham and cheese sandwiches

4 thick slices mature Cheddar or Gruyère cheese

8 pieces sourdough bread (Poilâne), sliced ½ inch thick

2 teaspoons Worcestershire sauce

4 slices good-quality ham

4 tablespoons butter

salt and freshly ground pepper

bread-and-butter pickles

1 pound Kirby cucumbers

2 small yellow onions, cut into thick rings

1¼ cups cider vinegar

2 cups sugar

1 tablespoon salt

1 tablespoon yellow mustard seeds

1 teaspoon celery seeds

3 sprigs fresh dill

1 teaspoon black peppercorns

potato chips and mustard, to serve

serves 4

To make the bread-and-butter pickles, slice the cucumbers ½ inch thick with a corrugated vegetable slicer or a regular knife. In a medium bowl, soak the onions and cucumber slices in ice water for 1 hour. Place all the remaining ingredients in a medium saucepan with ⅔ cup water and bring to a boil. Drain the cucumber and onions and put them in a large glass jar or sealable container. Pour the hot liquid over and let cool slightly before refrigerating. Chill for 24 hours before eating. Use within 1 week.

When you are ready to make the sandwiches, place the slices of Cheddar on 4 pieces of bread. Sprinkle each with ½ teaspoon Worcestershire sauce and top with a slice of ham. Cover each with a slice of bread. Spread 1 tablespoon of the butter on the outside of each sandwich. Give each a sprinkle of salt and pepper.

Heat a large, heavy, nonstick skillet. If you have only a small skillet, make the sandwiches in batches. Put the sandwiches in the skillet over medium/low heat for about 3–4 minutes on each side, or until brown. Cut each sandwich in half diagonally and serve warm. Serve with the Bread-and-Butter Pickles, potato chips, and your favorite mustard to dip in.

The meat in this Southern diner specialty is slow roasted, creating the juicy strings of pulled pork that make this sandwich so mouthwatering. Mix with your favorite barbecue sauce or try making the Smoky Barbecue Sauce on page 43.

pulled pork sandwiches

2¼ pounds boneless pork arm roast with fat on

3 tablespoons olive oil

2 teaspoons Spanish paprika (pimentón)

2 teaspoons dried oregano

1 teaspoon each salt and freshly ground pepper

1 cup favorite barbecue sauce, or Smoky Barbecue Sauce (page 43)

4 crusty white rolls

to serve

Three-seed Coleslaw with Sweet and Sour Dressing (page 51)

Bread-and-Butter Pickles (page 19)

serves 4

Preheat the oven to 250°F.

Rub the pork with 2 tablespoons of the olive oil and sprinkle with the paprika, oregano, salt, and pepper. Heat a nonstick skillet until very hot. Sear the pork on all sides and then place in a roasting pan. Cook for 5 hours.

Carefully remove the fat from the pork and shred the meat with two forks. Pour the barbecue sauce into a large skillet. Add the shredded meat and warm through over medium heat. When ready to serve, scoop the meat into the rolls and serve with the Three-seed Coleslaw with Sweet and Sour Dressing, and the Bread-and-Butter Pickles.

When a short-order cook is told to "burn one," a burger is flipped onto the grill. For the juiciest meat, avoid ground beef that is too lean. Ground sirloin is the best, but be sure it's marbled with fat to keep it from drying out when cooking.

hamburger with all the "fixins"

1 pound ground beef or ground sirloin

1 tablespoon Worcestershire sauce

½ teaspoon each of salt and freshly ground pepper

4 thick seeded buns or Kaiser rolls

fixins

4 tablespoons mayonnaise

yellow mustard and ketchup

4 pieces crisp iceberg lettuce

4 thin beefsteak tomato slices

16 pickle slices or peppadew peppers

4 paper-thin slices red onion

french fries, to serve

serves 4

In a medium bowl, mix the ground beef, Worcestershire sauce, salt, and pepper. Form into 4 equal burger patties.

Heat a grill pan or skillet until very hot. Lightly toast the buns and set aside. Season the burgers on both sides. Pan-fry the burgers over medium heat for about 3 minutes on each side for medium; cook slightly longer for well done. Alternatively, you can cook everything on an outdoor barbecue.

Spread the mayonnaise and a little mustard on the bottom of each bun. Lay down a piece of lettuce and top with a burger. Squirt some ketchup on each and top with the tomatoes, pickle, and onions. Top with the other side of the bun. Serve with french fries.

A CUP OF SOUP AND SALAD

Manhattan clam chowder is the tomato-based cousin of the creamy New England variety. Chowder fans still debate passionately over which is superior.

manhattan clam chowder

40 small clams

a handful of salt

3 ounces thick-sliced bacon, diced

1 large yellow onion, finely diced

1 celery rib, finely diced

2 garlic cloves, finely chopped

1 large carrot, peeled and finely diced

2 medium potatoes, peeled and cut into 1-inch chunks

two 14-ounce cans peeled and chopped plum tomatoes

2 bay leaves

1 cup clam juice or fish stock

¼ cup chopped fresh flatleaf parsley

salt and freshly ground pepper

oyster or saltine crackers, to serve

serves 4

Place the clams in a clean kitchen sink filled with very cold water and the salt. Leave for 30 minutes to draw out any impurities. Drain the clams and put them in a large, lidded pot. Add just enough water to cover by 2 inches. Cover with the lid and bring to a boil over high heat. Turn the heat down to low and cook for 1 minute. Remove the lid and, using a slotted spoon, set aside all the clams that have opened. Try reheating the ones that didn't open and discard any that still don't. Reserve the liquid and pass through a fine strainer. Leave the clams to cool slightly, then remove from their shells, roughly chop, and set aside. Alternatively, you can leave the clams in their shells.

In a large saucepan, pan-fry the bacon until crisp. Pour off most of the fat, leaving 2 tablespoons. Add the onion, celery, garlic, and carrot. Season and cook for 10 minutes. Add the potatoes, tomatoes, bay leaves, reserved clam liquid, and clam juice. Bring to a boil and cook for a further 10 minutes. Add the clams and parsley and taste for additional seasoning. Serve with oyster or saltine crackers.

The trick to producing rich stock is to brown the chicken first and cover while simmering. The result is a deep, flavorful base that suits any additions. Fine egg noodles are classic, but you can try rice or matzo balls.

chicken noodle soup

2 tablespoons olive oil

3 pounds chicken drumsticks and thighs

1 medium yellow onion, chopped

1 carrot, peeled and chopped

1 garlic clove, sliced

2 celery ribs, chopped

1 bouquet garni (bay leaf, thyme, and parsley)

to finish

1 medium yellow onion, chopped

2 large carrots, peeled and sliced ½ inch thick

2 celery ribs, sliced 1 inch thick

¼ cup finely chopped fresh flatleaf parsley

3 ounces fine egg noodles, broken into pieces

salt and freshly ground pepper

serves 4

Heat 1 tablespoon of the olive oil in a large, heavy stockpot. Season the chicken pieces and brown them in the pot in batches. Put all the chicken pieces back in the pot with the onion, carrot, garlic, and celery, and cook over low heat for 15 minutes. Pour in 6 cups water, add the bouquet garni, and simmer, covered, for 1 hour over medium/low heat. Remove any foamy scum from the surface during cooking.

Pour the finished stock through a fine strainer into a bowl and skim off any excess fat. Reserve the chicken and let cool before removing the meat from the bones and roughly chopping it.

To finish, heat the remaining olive oil in a saucepan. Add the onion, carrots, and celery, and season. Sauté for 5 minutes, then pour in the stock. Bring to a boil and add the noodles. Cook until the noodles are al dente, then add the chopped chicken. Sprinkle in the chopped parsley, stir, and serve.

cobb salad
with choice of dressings

Named after the owner of the Brown Derby restaurant in Hollywood, this composed salad has long been a favorite on diner menus. Try it with vinaigrette or one of the dressings below.

Heat the olive oil in a heavy, nonstick pan. Season the chicken and cook for 5–10 minutes on each side over medium/low heat, or until the juices run clear. Take off the heat and let sit for 5 minutes before removing any fat and thinly slicing the meat. Line a platter with the leaves of the baby Bibb. Arrange the chicken in a small stack and place the avocado next to it. Compose the other ingredients in piles. Serve with one of the dressings below.

1 tablespoon olive oil

4 large chicken breasts with skin on

4 heads baby Bibb lettuce, leaves separated

2 avocados, pitted, peeled, and cut into 1-inch pieces

½ iceberg lettuce, cut into chunks

1 large bunch watercress, stems removed

8 bacon slices, cooked

12 soft-cooked quails' eggs or 3 eggs

2 cups halved baby plum tomatoes

½ cup crumbled blue cheese

serves 4

catalina dressing

⅔ cup pure vegetable oil

¼ cup ketchup

¼ cup cider vinegar

3 tablespoons sugar

2 tablespoons grated onion

1 teaspoon Worcestershire sauce

½ teaspoon each salt and freshly ground pepper

Put the ingredients in a blender and purée until smooth. Refrigerate until ready to use.

italian dressing

¼ cup red wine vinegar

⅔ cup extra virgin olive oil

1 teaspoon sugar

1 garlic clove, bruised but left whole

1 tablespoon grated Parmesan cheese

½ teaspoon each salt and freshly ground pepper

1 teaspoon Dijon mustard

Put the ingredients in a small jar with a fitted lid and shake to combine.

green goddess dressing

½ cup mayonnaise

¼ cup sour cream

3 tablespoons chopped flatleaf parsley

1 tablespoon snipped chives

3 tablespoons chopped tarragon

2 tablespoons chopped onion

1 tablespoon red wine vinegar

2 anchovies, rinsed and chopped

Put the ingredients in a blender and purée until smooth. Refrigerate until ready to use.

DISH OF THE DAY

Crabcakes are the pride and joy of Mid-Atlantic diners, which have access to fresh, local seafood. They are perfect served with flavored fresh tomato salsa, mayonnaise, or cocktail sauce.

maryland crabcakes

12 ounces lump crabmeat

1 small red onion, finely diced

1 teaspoon Dijon mustard

1 teaspoon dried red pepper flakes

1½ cups fresh, fine bread crumbs, toasted

½ cup mayonnaise

1 egg, beaten

3 tablespoons finely chopped fresh flatleaf parsley

1 tablespoon grated peel from 1 unwaxed lemon

1 teaspoon Tabasco Sauce

½ cup pure vegetable or peanut oil

salt and freshly ground pepper

lemon or lime wedges, to serve

serves 4

Drain the crabmeat, squeezing out any excess liquid with your hands. Put it in a large mixing bowl with the red onion, mustard, red pepper flakes, ¾ cup of the bread crumbs, mayonnaise, egg, parsley, lemon peel, Tabasco, and seasoning. Combine the mixture with your hands and shape into 16 small or 12 medium-size cakes. Dip each cake into the remaining bread crumbs and chill for at least 30 minutes—this will help the crabcakes to stay firm when they are fried.

Preheat the oven to 300°F.

Heat the oil in a large, heavy skillet until moderately hot. Cook the crabcakes in batches of 4 for 2 minutes on each side. Don't let the oil get too hot or they will burn before the inside cooks. Drain on a baking sheet lined with paper towels and keep warm in the oven. Continue frying until all the crabcakes are finished. They can be made a half hour before serving and kept warm in the oven. Serve with lemon or lime wedges.

They didn't make pot pies with tarragon and sherry vinegar back in the fifties but it does make a tasty riff on this traditional comfort food. Sour cream and cornstarch make a creamy base that beats the customary white béchamel sauce.

chicken pot pies

13 ounces ready rolled puff pastry

16 small pearl onions, unpeeled

3 tablespoons olive oil

8 boneless, skinless chicken thighs, cut into 1-inch chunks

3 shallots, peeled and sliced

4 medium carrots, peeled and cut into 1½-inch chunks

¼ cup sherry vinegar

1½ cups dry white wine

1 cup sour cream

1 teaspoon cornstarch dissolved in 1 tablespoon water

1–2 sprigs fresh tarragon, stems removed and leaves chopped

salt and freshly ground pepper

four 5-inch ovenproof bowls or ramekins

serves 4

Preheat the oven to 400°F.

Unroll the pastry and cut out four 5½-inch circles to cover your bowls. Refrigerate the pastry circles until needed. Put the onions in a roasting pan and drizzle with 1 tablespoon of the olive oil. Roast for 15 minutes, remove from the oven, let cool, then slip off the peel, and set aside. Heat the remaining olive oil in a medium saucepan. Season and brown the chicken evenly, and remove from the pan.

Add the shallots and carrots to the saucepan, and season. Sauté over medium/low heat for 8 minutes. Pour in the vinegar and reduce by half. Add the chicken, onions, wine, sour cream, cornstarch, and chopped tarragon and cook for 5 minutes over medium/high heat.

Divide the mixture between the bowls. Place a pastry circle over each, press down over the sides of the bowl and make a ¾-inch slash in the center of the pastry to let the steam out. Bake for 20 minutes on a baking sheet. Let cool for 5 minutes and then serve.

Diners and truck stops sustain workers on the early or late shift. This "hungry man special" is a popular favorite for those with large appetites.

truck-stop steak with mushroom sauce

4 small ribeye or other steaks

2 tablespoons Worcestershire sauce

2 teaspoons olive oil

2 shallots, finely diced

1 garlic clove, finely chopped

2 cups small white button mushrooms, trimmed and halved

3 tablespoons red wine vinegar

⅓ cup red wine

1 tablespoon Dijon mustard

2 tablespoons chopped fresh flatleaf parsley

salt and freshly ground pepper

serves 4

Sprinkle the steaks with the Worcestershire sauce, and season. Heat 1 teaspoon of the olive oil in a heavy skillet until very hot. Add the steaks, sear for 3–4 minutes on each side, then wrap in aluminum foil to keep warm.

Wipe any burnt bits from the skillet and add the remaining olive oil. Sauté the shallots, garlic, and mushrooms over medium/high heat. Season and stir for about 5 minutes until soft. Add the vinegar, red wine, and mustard, and cook for a further 5 minutes over medium/high heat. Remove from the heat, pour over the steaks, and sprinkle with the parsley.

Chunks of tender steak and puréed dried chilies make this mouthwatering version of chili a bit more special.

a bowl of red

2¼ pounds chuck eye or boneless shoulder steak, cut into 1¾-inch chunks

1 bottle beer

4 ancho chilies, stemmed and seeded

6 tablespoons olive oil

2 large yellow onions, roughly chopped

6 garlic cloves, finely chopped

two 14-ounce cans whole, peeled plum tomatoes

¼ cup cider vinegar

¼ cup packed brown sugar

1 tablespoon mild chili powder

1 tablespoon Spanish paprika (preferably pimentón)

3 tablespoons cumin seeds, toasted and ground

14-ounce can kidney, Great Northern, or pinto beans, drained and rinsed

salt and freshly ground pepper

serves 4–6

Put the beef in a medium bowl, pour the beer over, and marinate for 30 minutes. Drain, reserving the liquid, and pat the beef dry with paper towels. Toast the chilies for 30 seconds in a dry sauté pan then pour boiling water over and soak for 15 minutes or until soft. Drain and put in a food processor with the beer. Purée until fine and set aside.

In a large saucepan, heat 2 tablespoons of the olive oil. Season the meat and sear in batches until evenly brown. Remove from the pan and set aside. Add the remaining olive oil and sauté the onions and garlic for 5 minutes. Put the meat back in the pan and pour the chili mixture over.

Purée the tomatoes in the food processor and add to the pan. Add the cider vinegar, brown sugar, chili powder, paprika, and cumin, and season. Cook, partially covered with a lid, for 1 hour over low heat or until the meat is very tender. Add the beans in the last 5 minutes of cooking to warm through. Serve in small bowls with your choice of accompaniments: cooked rice, chopped red onion, cilantro, or crackers.

1/4 cup olive oil

2 medium yellow onions, finely chopped

1 medium carrot, finely chopped

1 celery rib, finely chopped

1/2 cup milk

1 1/4 cups fresh bread crumbs

1/3 cup ketchup

2 teaspoons Worcestershire sauce

1 egg, beaten

1/2 cup chopped fresh flatleaf parsley

14 ounces coarsely ground beef

14 ounces coarsely ground pork

14-ounce can chopped tomatoes

2 teaspoons chopped fresh thyme

salt and freshly ground pepper

a loaf pan, 10 x 5 inches

serves 4

Chopped tomatoes and ketchup are poured over this meatloaf before cooking to keep it juicy and provide a tangy sauce for the accompanying mashed potatoes. If you don't have a loaf pan, roll the meatloaf mixture into a 10- x 5-inch shape on a foil-lined baking sheet.

mama's meatloaf

Preheat the oven to 400°F.

Heat the olive oil in a large sauté pan. Add the onions, carrot, and celery, and season. Sauté for 5 minutes then pour into a large mixing bowl. In a separate bowl, pour the milk over the bread crumbs and mix together. Add half the ketchup, the Worcestershire sauce, egg, parsley, bread crumb mixture, and the meats to the large mixing bowl.

Gently combine everything with your hands until well blended. Line the loaf pan with parchment paper and pack the mixture into it. Mix the tomatoes with the remaining ketchup and pour over the meatloaf. Sprinkle with salt and pepper and thyme. Bake for 1 hour, remove from the oven, and let stand for 10 minutes. Serve in thick slices with mashed potatoes.

This uncomplicated pomodoro sauce relies upon using the best canned Italian peeled plum tomatoes you can find. The milk-soaked bread and Parmesan keep the meatballs feather-light and impossible to stop eating.

spaghetti and meatballs

14 ounces ground pork or beef

1 small yellow onion, very finely chopped

1 egg, beaten

5 garlic cloves, finely chopped

3 tablespoons chopped fresh flatleaf parsley

3 tablespoons grated Parmesan cheese, plus extra, to serve

1 teaspoon each salt and freshly ground pepper

2 slices white bread

3 tablespoons milk

5 tablespoons olive oil

three 14-ounce cans whole, peeled plum tomatoes

1 tablespoon butter

14 ounces uncooked spaghetti

1 garlic clove, finely chopped

serves 4

Preheat the oven to 400°F.

In a medium bowl, combine the pork, onion, egg, most of the garlic, parsley, Parmesan cheese, salt, and pepper. Put the bread slices in a small bowl and pour over the milk. Break the mixture up into small pieces then add to the bowl with the meat. Mix everything with your hands until well combined. Roll into 2-inch balls and place on a baking sheet lined with parchment paper or aluminum foil. Bake for 15 minutes, giving the meatballs a shake halfway through cooking so they don't stick. Set aside.

In a large, wide saucepan, heat the olive oil and cook the remaining garlic until golden but not brown. Add the tomatoes and break up with a flat spoon. Season. Cook over medium/high heat for 15 minutes, stirring every 5 minutes or so. Keep a splatter screen on while cooking. The sauce should be thick when it is done. Add the butter and the meatballs.

Boil the spaghetti in plenty of salted water until it is just al dente. Drain and mix with the sauce. Serve sprinkled with grated Parmesan cheese.

1½ teaspoons chili powder

1 teaspoon garlic salt

1 tablespoon sugar

1 teaspoon each salt and freshly ground pepper

3 large racks of pork spareribs, preferably baby ones

smoky barbecue sauce

1 tablespoon olive oil

1 small yellow onion, diced

2 garlic cloves, chopped

2 bacon slices, chopped

14-ounce can peeled plum tomatoes, puréed

¼ cup tomato paste

¾ cup cider vinegar

½ cup packed brown sugar

2 tablespoons chili powder

2 teaspoons celery salt

3 tablespoons Worcestershire sauce

1 tablespoon yellow mustard

2 teaspoons Spanish paprika (pimentón)

1 tablespoon chopped chipotle chilies in adobo, or Tabasco Sauce

serves 4

This "rack of pig," as seasoned waitresses call it, is spice rubbed and then slow roasted until the meat is falling from the bone. Mexican chilies give the sauce a gorgeous smoky taste and a kick of heat.

sugar-rubbed babyback ribs with smoky barbecue sauce

Preheat the oven to 300°F.

In a small bowl, mix together the chili powder, garlic salt, sugar, salt, and pepper. Sprinkle the racks of pork on both sides with the mixture, put on a baking sheet, and cook for 1½ hours.

In the meantime, make the smoky barbecue sauce. Heat the olive oil in a medium saucepan. Sauté the onion, garlic, and bacon, for 5 minutes, or until soft. Add the remaining ingredients and cook for 10 minutes. If you are not using it straightaway, let cool and refrigerate in a sealed container.

Just before you are ready to serve the ribs, light your barbecue or preheat a gas grill. Brush the ribs on both sides with the fresh barbecue sauce. Grill for 5 minutes on each side or until crispy around the edges.

Mac and cheese is a firm comfort food favorite. Here it's given a modern makeover with upmarket cheeses like mascarpone and Parmesan, and a touch of garlic. The crisp topping rounds out the texture, making it live up to its name.

wicked mac and cheese

½ cup fresh, chunky bread crumbs

1 tablespoon olive oil

2 tablespoons butter

1 garlic clove, finely chopped

1 teaspoon dry mustard

3 tablespoons all-purpose flour

2 cups whole milk

½ cup mascarpone

1 cup grated mature Cheddar cheese

½ cup grated Parmesan cheese

12 ounces uncooked rigatoni or macaroni

a baking dish, 8 x 8 inches, or 4 ramekins

serves 4

Preheat the oven to 400°F.

Spread the bread crumbs on a baking sheet, drizzle with the oil, and season. Bake for 6 minutes, remove, and set aside.

Melt the butter in a medium saucepan. Add the garlic and mustard and sauté for 1 minute before adding the flour. Beat constantly over medium heat until it forms a paste. Gradually beat in the milk and turn up the heat. Bring to a boil, beating constantly. Turn the heat down to low and simmer for 10 minutes. Remove from the heat and add the mascarpone, Cheddar, and half of the Parmesan.

Boil the pasta in salted water until just al dente, drain, and mix with the cheese sauce. Season and spoon the mixture into the baking dish or ramekins. Top with the bread crumbs and the remaining Parmesan. Bake for 20 minutes until golden. Let sit for 5 minutes before serving.

EXTRAS

maple baked beans

Known as "brown bellies," these tremendous baked beans make the perfect sidekick for ribs or pulled pork sandwiches—or they are unashamedly good eaten on their own.

3 tablespoons olive oil

3 garlic cloves, chopped

1 large yellow onion, chopped

1 red bell pepper, seeded and diced

1 cup good-quality barbecue sauce

2 tablespoons yellow mustard

2 tablespoons cider vinegar

two 14-ounce cans Great Northern or pinto beans, drained

¼ cup maple syrup

6 bacon slices

salt and freshly ground pepper

serves 4

Preheat the oven to 325°F. In a heavy, ovenproof casserole dish, heat the oil. Add the garlic, onion, and red pepper, and season. Sauté for 5 minutes. Add the barbecue sauce, ½ cup water, the mustard, vinegar, beans, and maple syrup. Mix together, then lay the bacon slices over everything. Bake in the oven for 45 minutes. Let rest for 5 minutes, break up the bacon into bite-size pieces, and serve.

onion rings

Vidalia or other supersweet onions are best for this fried indulgence. You won't need a deep fat fryer; just a wok or small, heavy pot.

4–5 Vidalia or other large, sweet onions

3 egg whites

1 cup all-purpose flour

1 teaspoon each salt, freshly ground pepper, and chili powder

3 cups very fine, dry bread crumbs

2 cups peanut or pure vegetable oil

serves 4

Peel the onions and cut them into ½-inch slices. Break them up into rings, keeping the larger ones and discarding the smaller centers. Soak the large rings in a bowl of ice water for 1 hour and drain.

Beat the egg whites until they form soft peaks. In a separate bowl, combine the flour, salt, pepper, and chili powder, and add 1 cup water. Mix well. Fold in the egg whites until well combined. Put the bread crumbs in a shallow dish. Line a baking sheet with parchment paper or aluminum foil.

Dip the rings in the batter and then in the bread crumbs. Coat all the rings before you start frying. Heat the oil in a wok or heavy, medium saucepan. Drop a small piece of bread in the oil—if it sizzles the oil is hot enough. If not, heat it for a further minute or two before you start frying. Fry the onions a few at a time, for 2–3 minutes each. Drain on paper towels and sprinkle with salt.

au gratin potatoes

These are a bit different from potatoes "dauphinois," where raw potatoes are baked in cream. Here, the potatoes are boiled then baked with Cheddar and cream until golden and crusty.

4 large, floury potatoes, unpeeled
2 tablespoons olive oil
1 garlic clove, finely chopped
1 medium onion, finely chopped
1½ cups grated Cheddar cheese
⅓ cup grated Parmesan cheese
½ cup sour cream
½ cup whole milk
salt and freshly ground pepper

4 ramekins or a small baking dish

serves 4

Preheat the oven to 325°F.

Boil the potatoes in salted water until soft but still firm. Drain, peel, and cut into 1-inch chunks. Heat the oil in a medium skillet. Add the garlic and onion, season, and sauté for 5 minutes until soft.

Mix together the sour cream and milk in a medium bowl. Add the potatoes, onion mixture, and cheeses, and mix gently. Grease the ramekins or baking dish. Pour the potatoes in and cook for 45 minutes. Let sit for 10 minutes before serving.

thyme oven fries

If you boil or steam potato chunks before baking, you will get a result that's not far off the real thing.

1¾ pounds baking potatoes or sweet potatoes, unpeeled
6 tablespoons olive oil
1 teaspoon each salt and freshly ground pepper
2 teaspoons finely chopped fresh thyme

serves 4

Preheat the oven to 400°F.

Cut the potatoes into 1-inch slices. Slice these into 1-inch sticks. Bring a large saucepan of salted water to a boil and blanch the potatoes for 3 minutes. Drain well and spread the potatoes out on two baking sheets. Drizzle the oil over the potatoes and sprinkle with the salt, pepper, and fresh thyme. Bake for 20 minutes until golden. Turn the potatoes regularly while cooking to keep them from sticking.

three-seed coleslaw with sweet and sour dressing

Although mayonnaise-based coleslaw is irresistible, the lighter, healthier sweet and sour allows the cabbage's sweetness and crunch to shine through.

¼ red cabbage, thinly sliced

¼ green cabbage, thinly sliced

1 large red bell pepper, seeded and finely diced

2 medium carrots, cut into thin matchsticks

1 small yellow onion, diced

dressing

¼ cup sugar

¼ cup cider vinegar

½ cup pure vegetable oil

½ teaspoon each mustard seeds, celery seeds, and poppy seeds

1 teaspoon dry mustard powder

½ teaspoon each salt and freshly ground pepper

serves 4

In a large bowl, soak the vegetables in ice water for 1 hour, then drain and dry on a clean kitchen towel.

For the dressing, put the ingredients in a small saucepan and bring to a boil. Cook for 1 minute until syrupy then set aside to cool slightly. In a large bowl, mix the vegetables and dressing. Refrigerate for a half hour before serving.

potato salad

The secret to this tangy side dish is to toss the potatoes in vinegar while they are still warm. Organic eggs, with their bright yellow yolks, keep the color of this salad vibrant.

1¾ pounds medium potatoes

5 tablespoons red wine vinegar

½ teaspoon each salt and freshly ground pepper

¾ cup mayonnaise

2 small, sweet pickles, finely diced

2 tablespoons Dijon mustard

1 medium yellow onion, finely diced

2 celery ribs, finely diced

2 hard-cooked eggs, preferably organic, sliced

serves 4

Boil the potatoes in salted water until soft but still firm. Drain and let cool slightly. In a large bowl, combine the vinegar, salt, and pepper. Slice the potatoes into 1-inch chunks and combine with the vinegar. Refrigerate for 20 minutes.

Meanwhile, mix the mayonnaise, pickles, mustard, onion, celery, and eggs together. Toss the cold potatoes with the dressing, season, and refrigerate until ready to use.

SOMETHIN' FROM THE SWEET COUNTER

4 small bananas

4 scoops each of strawberry, vanilla, and chocolate ice cream

4 maraschino cherries

½ cup chopped, toasted pecans

hot fudge sauce

3 ounces semisweet chocolate, chopped

¾ cup heavy cream

2 tablespoons butter

¼ cup light corn syrup

1 teaspoon pure vanilla extract

½ cup sugar

whipped cream

1 cup heavy cream

1 tablespoon superfine sugar

1 teaspoon pure vanilla extract

four banana split dishes

serves 4

Order a banana split at your local diner and the waitress is likely to ask the cook to build a "houseboat" or a "Dagwood special." Whatever you call it, it's a beloved ice cream creation.

banana splits with hot fudge sauce

To make the hot fudge sauce, put the chocolate, cream, and butter in a medium saucepan. When melted, add the light corn syrup, vanilla extract, and the sugar, stirring constantly over medium heat. When nearly boiling, turn the heat down to low and simmer for 15 minutes without stirring. Let cool for 5 minutes before using.

To make the whipped cream, beat the heavy cream with the sugar and vanilla, and set aside. Peel the bananas and cut in half lengthwise. Take the dessert dishes and along the sides of each one, put 2 banana halves. Put one scoop of each flavor of ice cream between the bananas. Top with one spoonful of the whipped cream, a sprinkling of pecans, and a cherry on top. Serve with a small pitcher of the hot fudge sauce to pour over.

A dessert case fixture, devil's food cake has a fine-crumbed texture and meringue-like frosting that both melt in the mouth.

devil's food counter cake with 7-minute frosting

1½ cups boiling water

1 cup unsweetened cocoa powder

4 eggs (at room temperature)

1 tablespoon pure vanilla extract

3½ cups cake flour

1 teaspoon salt

1 teaspoon baking soda

2¼ cups sugar

1½ cups unsalted butter, softened

7-minute frosting

1¼ cups sugar

2 egg whites (at room temperature)

1½ tablespoons light corn syrup

¼ teaspoon cream of tartar

¼ teaspoon salt

1 teaspoon pure vanilla extract

three 8-inch cake pans or two 9-inch

serves 8–10

Preheat the oven to 350°F. Grease the cake pans and line them with waxed paper. Grease the paper, then dust with flour, and shake off any excess.

Beat together the boiling water and cocoa in a medium bowl until smooth. Let cool until it is at room temperature. When it is cool, beat together the eggs, vanilla extract, and ⅓ cup of the cocoa mixture.

Sift the flour, salt, and baking soda into the bowl of an electric mixer, and stir in the sugar. Mix on low speed for 30 seconds, then add the softened butter and remaining cocoa liquid. Mix on low speed then turn up to medium and beat for 1½ minutes. Add the egg mixture in 3 batches, beating each one for 30 seconds. Don't overbeat or the cake will be heavy. Scrape the batter into the cake pans and smooth the surfaces.

Put 2 cakes in the middle of the oven and 1 in the lower part. Bake for 25–30 minutes or until a skewer inserted into the center of the cake comes out clean. Rotate the cakes halfway through cooking. Let cool in the pans for 10 minutes then turn out onto wire racks, remove the paper, and let cool completely. Wrap in plastic wrap for up to 2 days before frosting.

To make the frosting, put 6 tablespoons water and all ingredients except the vanilla extract in a large glass bowl. Put the bowl over a saucepan of simmering water (the bottom of the bowl shouldn't touch the water). Beat with an electric beater on high speed for 7 minutes. Remove from the heat, add the vanilla extract, and beat for 2 minutes more, until stiff and glossy.

Put 1 cake on a plate. Secure the cake with a bit of frosting underneath. Top with about ½ cup of the frosting. Place another cake on top and spread another ½ cup of frosting over. Top with the last cake, frost the sides, and finish with the top. Use the back of a spoon to create peaks in the frosting. The cake can sit, covered, at room temperature, for up to 2 days.

Traditional cheesecakes are often served with a thick fruit sauce, like blueberries or cherries, on top, but this cheesecake's dense, creamy texture can stand on its own.

new york cheesecake

7 ounces graham crackers or chocolate wafers

4 tablespoons melted butter

36 ounces cream cheese

1 cup sugar

grated peel and freshly squeezed juice of 1 unwaxed lemon

1 cup sour cream

2 tablespoons pure vanilla extract

5 eggs

¼ cup all-purpose flour

a springform cake pan, 8-inch diameter

serves 8–10

Preheat the oven to 275°F.

Crush the graham crackers in a food processor then add the melted butter and mix well. Press the mixture firmly into the cake pan. Bake for 5 minutes, remove, and let cool. Grease the sides of the pan above the crust.

In a large bowl, beat the cream cheese and sugar with an electric beater. Add the lemon peel, juice, sour cream, and vanilla extract. Mix until smooth and add the eggs one at a time until well combined. Put the flour in last and mix again. Pour the mixture into the cake pan. Bake for 70 minutes until it is firm and the top is turning light golden. Let sit in the oven with the door open until cool (about 2 hours), then refrigerate for at least 6 hours or overnight. Place your favorite fresh fruit on top and serve.

For the best flaky pastry, freeze the butter and shortening before making the dough and use a pie dish made of glass. When combining, be sure to get the flour and butters to the crumb stage before mixing in the water.

basic pie crust

1¼ cups all-purpose flour

a pinch of salt

6 tablespoons unsalted butter, frozen

2 tablespoons pure vegetable shortening, frozen

1 egg white, to seal

a glass pie dish, 9-inch diameter

makes a 9-inch crust

Combine the flour and salt in a large bowl. Chop the shortening and butter into 1-inch pieces and add to the bowl. Using a pastry blender or two knives, chop through the mixture until it resembles coarse bread crumbs. Add 3 tablespoons ice water and bring the mixture together with a fork. Add additional water if necessary until it comes together with your hands. Very quickly knead the dough into a ball. Don't handle it for too long or it will become warm. Flatten the dough into a disk, cover in plastic wrap, and refrigerate for 1 hour.

To roll the dough, work on a large surface that is not near a warm stove or dishwasher. Sprinkle flour over the area and a rolling pin. Dust both sides of the dough with flour, and roll out. When it is 12 inches in diameter, gently and loosely wrap the dough around the rolling pin. Unwrap the dough over the pie dish and press it into the bottom and sides. Trim the edges leaving a 1-inch overhang. Turn the edges under and press to form a crust. Use your fingers to crimp it all around the edge of the dish. Place in the freezer for at least 30 minutes.

To bake the crust blind, preheat the oven to 400°F. Cover the chilled pastry with a large sheet of parchment paper. Fill with baking beans and bake for 15 minutes. Remove the paper and beans, brush the crust with the egg white, and bake for a further 8 minutes. Remove and let cool on a rack.

A selection of tempting pies is the pride of most diners. This one combines two favorites: coconut cream and banana cream. Brush egg white on the pie crust before baking to prevent any sogginess.

coconut and banana cream pie

1 recipe Basic Pie Crust (page 58)

1¼ cups shredded coconut

⅔ cup sugar

¼ cup cornstarch

a pinch of salt

1¼ cups coconut milk

¾ cup whole milk

1 fresh vanilla bean, split

5 large egg yolks

3 tablespoons butter, cut into pieces

topping

3 small, ripe bananas, sliced 1 inch thick

1 teaspoon freshly squeezed lemon juice

1½ cups heavy cream

1 teaspoon pure vanilla extract

2 tablespoons sugar

serves 8

Preheat the oven to 350°F.

Spread the shredded coconut on a baking sheet. Bake for 6 minutes then remove to cool. In a medium saucepan, combine the sugar, cornstarch, and salt. Beat in the coconut milk and whole milk until smooth. Scrape the seeds out from the vanilla bean and put in the saucepan along with the bean. Cook over medium heat and bring to a boil, beating constantly. Remove from the heat and take out the vanilla bean.

In a medium bowl, beat the egg yolks. Add a small amount of the hot mixture to the egg yolks and beat. Pour in the remaining mixture, beat again, and pour everything back into the saucepan. Cook over medium/high heat, beating constantly until it boils. Boil for 1 minute, then remove from the heat. Beat in the butter until incorporated and add 1 cup of the shredded coconut. Let cool for 20 minutes and then pour into the cooked pie crust. Lay a piece of plastic wrap on the surface of the pie filling and refrigerate for at least 3 hours.

To make the topping, toss the banana slices in the lemon juice. Beat the cream with the vanilla extract and sugar until it forms soft peaks. Remove the plastic wrap from the pie, arrange a thin layer of bananas over the top, and spread the cream over. Sprinkle the remaining shredded coconut over the top. Refrigerate until ready to serve.

Your efforts will be forgotten when you take your first bite of this wondrous pie. The lemon filling should be hot when topping with the meringue, as it steams the egg whites and ensures that they stay firm.

lemon meringue pie

1 recipe Basic Pie Crust
(page 58)

filling

1 scant cup granulated sugar

¼ cup cornstarch

a pinch of salt

5 egg yolks

½ cup freshly squeezed
lemon juice

1 tablespoon grated lemon peel

3 tablespoons unsalted butter

1 teaspoon pure vanilla extract

meringue

1 tablespoon cornstarch

5 egg whites

a pinch of salt

¼ teaspoon cream of tartar

½ cup superfine sugar

serves 8

Preheat the broiler. To make the filling, combine 1½ cups cold water, the granulated sugar, cornstarch, and salt in a saucepan. Over medium/high heat, bring the mixture to a boil, beating constantly. Remove from the heat. In a medium bowl, beat the egg yolks. Pour ½ cup of the sugar mixture into the egg yolks and beat well. Pour the yolk mixture back into the saucepan. Bring the mixture to a boil over medium/high heat, beating constantly. Boil for 1 minute then remove from the heat. Beat in the lemon juice, peel, and butter, and finally the vanilla extract. Let sit while you make the meringue.

To make the meringue, heat the cornstarch and ⅓ cup water in a small saucepan. Bring to a boil over medium/high heat, stirring constantly. Boil for 30 seconds and remove from the heat. In a large bowl, beat the egg whites with an electric beater on a low speed until they are frothy. Add the salt and cream of tartar, turn the speed up to medium/high, and beat until the whites form soft peaks. Add the sugar 1 spoonful at a time until the meringue is very glossy. Add a little of the meringue to the cornstarch mixture and stir. Pour this slowly back into the meringue and beat on high speed until stiff peaks form.

Reheat the lemon mixture until hot. Pour this into the pie crust. Gently spoon the meringue over the surface, making sure that it adheres to the crust and is well sealed. Use the back of a spoon to make decorative peaks and swirls on top. Put on a rack 4–6 inches below a very hot broiler for about 5 minutes, or until brown. Let cool completely on a rack, then refrigerate until ready to serve. Eat on the same day of preparation.

2 recipes Basic Pie Crust dough (page 58), uncooked

6 Granny Smith apples, peeled, cored, and sliced ¼ inch thick

6 Golden Delicious apples, peeled, cored, and sliced ¼ inch thick

2½ tablespoons cornstarch

1 teaspoon grated lemon peel

1 tablespoon freshly squeezed lemon juice

1 teaspoon ground cinnamon

¼ teaspoon ground cloves

½ teaspoon freshly grated nutmeg

½ teaspoon salt

¾ cup sugar plus 1 tablespoon

1 egg white

a glass pie dish, 9-inch diameter

serves 8

Known in diner slang as "Eve with a lid on," apple pie is a beloved favorite. Although most people think of it as American, it was first made in England and brought over by colonists.

apple pie

Roll out one portion of pie dough and arrange in the pie dish, following the instructions on page 58. Set aside. Roll out the other portion of dough until it is a 12-inch disk. Transfer to a piece of parchment paper. Place both in the refrigerator, leaving at least 1 hour before filling.

Preheat the oven to 375°F. Put a baking sheet inside to heat. To make the filling, toss the apples in a large mixing bowl with ¾ cup of the sugar, the cornstarch, lemon peel and juice, cinnamon, cloves, nutmeg, and salt. Pour into the uncooked pie crust and cover with the rolled pastry. Press the edges together to seal. Tuck the dough underneath itself and press onto the rim of the dish. Crimp the edges of pastry in a zigzag pattern. Cut 4 small slits in the pastry with a knife to let the steam out. Brush the top with the egg white and sprinkle over the remaining tablespoon of sugar. Bake the pie on the hot baking sheet for 60 minutes, or until golden brown.

8 large scoops chocolate ice cream

1 cup whole milk

½ cup thin chocolate-flavored syrup

serves 4

Chill your glasses in the freezer to keep the milkshake icy cold.

chocolate milkshake

Put all the ingredients in a blender and process until smooth. Pour into 4 glasses and serve.

index

conversion chart

Weights and measures have been rounded up or down slightly to make measuring easier.

Measuring butter:

A US stick of butter weighs 4 oz. which is approximately 115 g or 8 tablespoons. The recipes in this book require the following conversions:

American	Metric	Imperial
6 tbsp	85 g	3 oz.
7 tbsp	100 g	3½ oz.
1 stick	115 g	4 oz.

Volume equivalents:

American	Metric	Imperial
1 teaspoon	5 ml	
1 tablespoon	15 ml	
¼ cup	60 ml	2 fl.oz.
⅓ cup	75 ml	2½ fl.oz.
½ cup	125 ml	4 fl.oz.
⅔ cup	150 ml	5 fl.oz. (¼ pint)
¾ cup	175 ml	6 fl.oz.
1 cup	250 ml	8 fl.oz.

Weight equivalents: | | **Measurements:**

Imperial	Metric	Inches	cm
1 oz.	30 g	¼ inch	5 mm
2 oz.	55 g	½ inch	1 cm
3 oz.	85 g	1 inch	2.5 cm
3½ oz.	100 g	2 inches	5 cm
4 oz.	115 g	3 inches	7 cm
6 oz.	175 g	4 inches	10 cm
8 oz. (½ lb.)	225 g	5 inches	12 cm
9 oz.	250 g	6 inches	15 cm
10 oz.	280 g	7 inches	18 cm
12 oz.	350 g	8 inches	20 cm
13 oz.	375 g	9 inches	23 cm
14 oz.	400 g	10 inches	25 cm
15 oz.	425 g	11 inches	28 cm
16 oz. (1 lb.)	450 g	12 inches	30 cm

Oven temperatures:

120°C	(250°F)	Gas ½
140°C	(275°F)	Gas 1
150°C	(300°F)	Gas 2
170°C	(325°F)	Gas 3
180°C	(350°F)	Gas 4
190°C	(375°F)	Gas 5
200°C	(400°F)	Gas 6